I0070085

# FORWARD

This book has been written for the purpose of helping business owners better understand the business side of their business. After becoming familiar with the information contained in this book, the individual will find him or herself more knowledgeable in reference to the business rules that govern self-employed individuals and businesses.

This manual has been written with the understanding that it is not a legal document nor is it intended to replace the services one would receive from an Accountant, Attorney, or Tax Professional. Therefore, after familiarizing yourself with the information contained in this book, if you require additional assistance, please seek this assistance from an Accountant, Attorney, or Tax Professional.

K. L. Alston Enterprises, Publisher
K. L. Alston, Author

**Things You Should Know Before and After Starting a Business**

Copyright 2020 by K. L. Alston

# **Table of Contents**

# **INTRODUCTION**

As a business owner, it is to your advantage to familiarize yourself with the income tax rules as they apply to self-employed individuals. Although I am not advocating you have to become an expert in tax law, I am advocating you should have a clear understanding of what you can or cannot do, and what you are or are not entitled to. The income tax rules can work for you if they are properly understood and more importantly, properly utilized. However, the income tax rules can be a self-employed individual's worst nightmare if they are not.

In this manual, I will explain the different business structures available to you. I will also define business income and explain the different types of expenses you are allowed to deduct as business deductions and the conditions in which these expenses are deductible. I will also discuss record keeping, retirement planning, and a host of other pertinent information. Also included in this manual is a sample business Income Tax return along with sample blank IRS forms.

# DEFINITION OF A TRADE OR BUSINESS

A "Trade or Business" is characterized as an activity engaged in for livelihood or for profit. In order for an activity to be characterized as a "Trade or Business", *the intentions of making a profit and some type of economical activity must be present.* If the above two criteria are not met, the activity could be considered a "Hobby" by the IRS. Since it is not always easy to distinguish between a trade or business and a hobby, one important factor used to distinguish the two is the amount of time devoted by the taxpayer towards the activity. Based on the Court, *an activity in which the taxpayer engages in "full-time, in good faith, and with regularity, to the production of income or a livelihood and [which] is not a mere hobby" is considered a trade or business.* An important point to mention about a "Hobby" is that any income derived from it must be reported as income for income tax purposes. However, you cannot deduct any of the expenses you may incur from a hobby. So, it is particularly important the IRS does not reclassify your trade or business as a hobby.

## BUSINESS STRUCTURES (Legal Entities)

More and more people are starting businesses everyday. With the ever-changing economy, and the fluctuating job markets, having only one source of income is not such a great idea. Starting a business is an important decision, and as it is with any important decision, planning and organization are two important ingredients in the recipe for success. Since you have already decided to operate your own business, it is important to understand the various legal entities or forms of business structures available.

When deciding which business structure to utilize, there are many factors to consider. For example, the business structure you select will directly affect how your business expenses will be deducted and more importantly, your decision will serve as the basic foundation in developing an effective tax strategy that will govern your financial savings or your financial losses. *Remember, tax planning does not begin during the income tax preparation stage.* For those of you who have yet to structure your trade or business, this section will prove vital in your decision-making process. For those of you who have, this section may encourage you to change your already existing business structure. In this section, I will give a brief overview of Sole proprietorships, Partnerships, Corporations, and Limited Liability Companies.

## SOLE PROPRIETORSHIPS

When you establish a business and you are the sole owner of that business, and that business is not a corporation; you are considered a sole proprietor. For taxation purposes, the term "proprietor" means any trade or business owned by one person. It is fairly simple and inexpensive, from an accounting and legal perspective, to establish a sole proprietorship. All you need to do is simply operate your business.

However, although the accounting and legal costs may be nominal, the cost of "personal liability" could prove to be otherwise. As a sole proprietor, you are personally liable for any and all debts your business incurs. This means to satisfy a business debt, not only can a creditor go after your business assets (equipment and other business property); a creditor can also go after your personal assets as well if the business assets are not sufficient to cover the debt. As a sole proprietor, personal assets such as cash, stocks, bonds, real estate or even your homestead (your home and its property) become fair game when it comes to satisfying a business debt. However, the good news is, there are some states that protect your homestead against this type of liability. The not so good news, there are some states that do not. Therefore, as a sole proprietor, it is definitely within your best interest to find out if the state you are conducting your trade or business in does or does not protect your homestead. In general, the best protection besides paying your debts in full is the protection of adequate liability insurance coverage against accidents and other business liabilities. *So, as a sole proprietor, please insure you have sufficient liability insurance coverage to protect your business as well as yourself against accidents, legal actions, and other potential business liabilities.*

For income tax purposes, sole proprietors are required to pay their taxes in the form of estimated tax payments. Sole proprietors are required to report their income on Form Schedule C, Profit or Loss from Business or on Form Schedule C EZ, Net Profit from Business. You can not use the Form Schedule C EZ if your business expenses total more than $2,500.00, if your method of accounting is the accrual method, if you are planning to deduct expenses for the use of your home for business, if you have employees, if you have inventory, or if you have a net loss for the tax year. If you meet anyone of the conditions stated above, you will have to report your business income and expenses on the Form Schedule C, Profit or Loss from Business.

The net amount of income (the amount after all expenses have been deducted) is then transferred and reported on the taxpayer's Form 1040. If your total net profit totals $400.00 or more, you are required to pay into the Social Security System by filing the Form Schedule S E. Your total net profit or net loss is the total amount from all businesses. For example, if you are the sole proprietor of two businesses and one business has a net profit of $1,000.00 while the other has a net loss of $500.00, your total net profit is $500.00.

# INDEPENDENT CONTRACTOR

An independent contractor is also considered a form of sole proprietorship. For definition purposes, an independent contractor is anyone who provides a service to others outside the boundaries of an employee. Business owners as well as those working as independent contractors need to be careful because the IRS can be aggressive in its attempt to reclassify a worker as an employee in order to prevent employers from **not paying** employment taxes. To prove independent contractor status, it must be proven the independent contractor has the right to control the manner in which the work is to be accomplished. In other words, the issue of whether or not the independent contractor is under someone else's control regarding the work environment becomes an issue. It is also quite beneficial for the independent contractor if he or she furnishes his or her own supplies and equipment based upon the type of work being performed. A written contract would also be very instrumental if there is ever a discrepancy.

# PARTNERSHIPS

When you establish a business with the intent of sharing the profits or losses with a partner or partners, you are treated as being in a partnership. A partnership can be in the form of a *General Partnership or a Limited Partnership.* With a General Partnership, each partner is personally liable for the debts incurred by the partnership. Therefore, just as with a sole proprietorship, a creditor can go after the personal assets of each partner to satisfy a debt. However, in addition to *"personal-liability"*, in a general partnership all partners are *"jointly and severally liable"* for all partnership debts. *This means a creditor can go after anyone partner to recover the full amount of a debt incurred by the partnership.* In turn, that partner can seek repayment from the other partner or partners in the amount proportional to that partner's or partners' share of the collected debt.

With a Limited Partnership, the limited partner is only liable up to his or her investment, recourse debt (debt in which the partnership or at least one partner is liable for), and future obligations to make investments. Therefore, if the partnership debt is $30,000.00 and the limited partner has only invested $10,000.00, although the general partners are liable for the entire amount of the $30,000.00, the limited partner's share of the debt is only $10,000.00 providing the debt is not non-recourse debt (debt in which neither the partnership nor any partner is liable for) and there is no future obligation to make investments. In a limited partnership, since your liability is limited to your investment, so can your return on your investment be limited to your investment. Therefore, depending upon your partnership agreement, your return can be substantially less than that of the general partners.

For income tax purposes, partnerships are considered *"pass-through"* *entities.* This means the partnership itself does not pay any taxes although a partnership tax return is required (Form 1065). *The income, deductions, gains, losses, and credits are passed through to the partners who report these amounts on their personal income tax returns.* A partner in a partnership is required to pay self-employment taxes on his or her share of the business income. Partners are also required to make estimated tax payments as well.

Unlike a sole proprietorship, the accounting and legal costs of establishing a partnership may be somewhat more expensive. Most commonly, partnerships are organized with formal partnership agreements although verbal partnership agreements do exist. These formal partnership agreements detail everything from the distribution of income and deductions to what happens to the partnership at the death of a partner. Because of the potential complexity of a formal partnership agreement, the professional skills of an accountant and an attorney may be needed.

## CORPORATIONS

There are two types of corporations: **C *Corporations and* S *Corporations.*** Although these two entities are similar, there are some major differences. Both the C Corporation and the S Corporation provide what is called ***"Limited Liability."*** If you recall, with the sole proprietorship and the partnership, the owners are personally liable (Personal Liability) for any and all debts incurred by the business. This is not the case with a corporation. Because legally, a corporation is considered a totally separate and unique entity from its owners (shareholders), the owners (shareholders) are protected by limited liability. With limited liability, a creditor **cannot** go after the personal assets of the owners, (shareholders) however the assets of the corporation are fair game. Although there are special times when even the protection of limited liability does not protect you, such times are outside the parameter of this manual.

Both the C Corporation and the S Corporation are formed under state law therefore the rules for incorporating may vary depending upon the state. Although both the C Corporation (Form 1120) and the Sub S Corporation (Form 1120s) are required to submit income tax returns, this is where a major difference occurs. An S Corporation is taxed just like a partnership, as a *"pass-through" entity.* Therefore, the Sub S Corporation does not pay any income taxes although a tax return is filed. *The income, deductions, gains, losses, and credits are passed through to the owners (shareholders) who report these amounts on their personal income tax return.* In addition, self-employment taxes are not paid on the distribution of the income from the S Corporation. With a C Corporation, *"Double Taxation"* is a concern. With double taxation, the corporate income is taxed once at the corporate level in the form of income and again at the owners' (shareholders') level in the form of distributions called dividends. Both corporate business structures are effective depending upon what you wish to accomplish. This is why understanding these business structures is so important. Your business structure sets the foundation regarding your financial strategy.

## LIMITED LIABILITY COMPANY (LLC)

A Limited Liability Company (LLC) is formed under state law and can be classified as either a Partnership or a Corporation for federal income tax purposes. If it is classified as a corporation, it will abide by the same rules that govern the existence of a corporation for federal income tax purposes. On the other hand, if it is classified as a partnership, it will abide by the same rules that govern the existence of a partnership for federal income tax purposes. *The members of an LLC have the protection of limited liability, therefore; none of the members of an LLC are personally liable for the debts of the LLC. A creditor cannot go after the personal assets of a member of an LLC to satisfy a business debt.* Although there are special times when even the protection of limited liability does not protect you, such times are outside the parameter of this manual. For income tax purposes, the same income tax forms used to prepare either the return of a partnership (Form 1065) or a corporation (1120) is used to prepare the return of an LLC. The appropriate tax forms will be based upon the classification of the LLC.

# EMPLOYER IDENTIFICATION NUMBER

If you have employees and are required to give tax statements, or are required to report employment taxes, you need an employer identification number. The employer identification number is a nine-digit number issued by the IRS. The number is very much similar in use to a social security number. The IRS to identify a business utilizes it. Just as no two people have the same social security number, no two businesses have the same employer identification number. The Form SS-4 is the form submitted to the IRS to request an employer identification number. A business should have only one Employer Identification Number. If you take over another business, do not use the original Employer Identification Number. Apply for a different number. One of the questions you will encounter while preparing the Form SS-4 is what type of business structure do you have?

# BUSINESS CHECKING ACCOUNT

One of the first lines of business when starting a business is to establish a banking account for your business. This is the case even if your business structure is a sole proprietorship. Most banking institutions require that a business have an employer identification number to establish an account with them. An employer identification number is issued by the IRS and is applied for by submitting a completed Form SS-4. You will notice when you are completing the Form SS-4 that one of the questions pertains to the type of business structure you are establishing.

It is not appropriate to inter-mingle business funds with personal funds. This means you should establish a separate checking account to account for your business income and expenses. This concept may appear much clearer when it comes to a partnership, corporate, or LLC type business structure. Reason being, these types of business structures normally involve more than one person, and the start-up rules are more complex. However, with a sole proprietorship the intermingling of funds is an all too often occurrence. Due to its simplicity in reference to start-up, many individuals feel it much simpler to just deposit the business income into an already existing personal checking account. The task of accounting for business income and recording business expenses becomes a much easier task when the business has its own banking account. It eliminates the question of which part of this balance is personal income and which part of it is business income. With business accounting software, you fully enter each check written and during the posting process, the appropriate accounts are debited and credited. In addition, checks make the best receipts. Years later you can contact the bank from which the check was drawn and request a copy of the check. With a cash receipt if you happen to lose it, you may find it very difficult to get a replacement copy of that receipt to substantiate the expense, so as often as possible write business checks when making purchases for your business.

## STATE TAX AGENCY REQUIREMENTS

Depending upon the state in which you start and operate your business, more than- likely there are certain filing requirements that should be met prior to operating your business. Filing requirements such as applying for an employer withholding identification number, a state tax identification number, and a state unemployment tax identification number, etc. For your convenience, in the back of the manual I have included a listing of the state tax offices for each state. The listing includes the address and phone number of each office. If you are unsure, contact the appropriate office for your state, and find out what the filing requirements are for starting or operating a business.

## BUSINESS INCOME

Business income is income received by your business from the sale of products or services. As stated earlier, if your business income results in net earnings of $400.00 or more, the Form Schedule S E (Schedule used to compute the self-employment tax) must be utilized to compute the self-employment tax, which is the combination of the social security and Medicare tax imposed on self-employed individuals. For a better understanding of social security taxes, I will explain the two systems under which social security taxes are collected: FICA and SECA. Under the Federal Insurance Contributions Act (FICA), the employee pays a portion of the social security tax, and the employer pays the other portion of the social security tax. Under the self-employment Contributions Act (SECA), the self-employed individual pays the entire tax amount. No earnings are subject to both systems simultaneously.

In reference to reporting business income, there are generally two methods of accounting that govern when and how you report business income. One is the Cash Method and the other is the Accrual Method. Under the cash method, your business income is considered income after you have received the payment for a product, or a service rendered. Under the accrual method, your business income is considered earned income after you have delivered that product or service, even if you have not physically collected the money. Therefore, under the accrual method you have to include in your business income the amount for the product or the service you have provided even if you have not received the payment for that product or service you provided. You generally have the option to choose the method you wish to utilize.

# BARTERING INCOME

Bartering occurs when goods or services are exchanged without the exchange of money. An example of bartering is an Accountant performing income tax work for an Attorney in exchange for legal services. Both parties involved in the bartering transaction must include in their business income the fair market value of the goods or services exchanged. Fair market value is the current monetary value of an object or a service at a specified moment in time.

Income you receive from bartering is taxable in the year in which the goods or services were received. In addition, the expenses incurred as a result of the barter transaction are also deductible by you in the year in which the transaction occurred. If you are involved in a barter exchange, you should receive or provide a Form ten-ninety-nine-B, Proceeds from Broker and Barter Exchange Transactions. This form will generally display the value any cash, property, services or credits you received from the exchange.

# PETTY CASH FUND

For the payment of various small office expenditures such as cab fare, postage, highway tolls, parking, small office supplies and similar expenditures, a petty cash fund can be utilized. A petty cash fund is an excellent way to keep track of the receipts for small incidental business expenditures. Quite simply the receipts, plus the cash on-hand, should always equal the amount of money that was initially in the petty cash fund. If this is not the case, funds from the petty cash fund have been spent, however it has not been accounted for by replacing the amount spent with the appropriate receipt or receipts. Once the petty cash fund has been fully utilized, or down to a predetermined amount, the petty cash fund can be replenished, and the receipts accounted for, recorded, and placed in a safe place for filing.

## EXPENSES

There are three rules an expense must meet to be deductible as a trade or business expense and they are as follows:

1.) The expense must be an ordinary and necessary expense of the business,
2.) The expense must be paid or incurred during the tax year in which it is deducted, *and*
3.) The expense has to be related to the business.

The term *"ordinary"* describes expenses that are normal for the taxpayer's business while the term *"necessary"* is used to distinguish an expense of the business from a personal expense incurred by the taxpayer. It is of the utmost importance to keep business expenses separate from personal expenses. Although *"necessary"* expenses need not be the determining factor if a business fails or succeeds, they have to be beneficial or helpful to the business.

## ADVERTISING EXPENSES

Advertising expenses must be related to the business. For example, the cost of business cards can be a deductible advertising expense. *Advertising expenses serve the purpose of exposing and keeping the business's name, products, or services before the public.* There are many different forms of advertisements, so you are free to choose the method of advertising that best serve the business. However, one important point to remember is that the burden of proving that the advertising expense incurred is a legitimate business expense is your responsibility

## AUTOMOBILE EXPENSES

Just like any other business expense, automobile expenses must meet the following criteria for it to be a legitimate deduction.

1.) The expense must be ordinary and necessary, *and*

2,) The expense must be incurred in the business of the taxpayer.

To calculate the amount of car expenses deductible, you can utilize either the ***standard-mileage-rate method or the actual-cost method.*** The taxpayer is generally free to use whichever method yields the largest deduction. However, an important rule to remember is the standard-mileage-rate method can only be used in the current year if this method was used in the first year the automobile was placed in service for trade or business purposes. Further, if you utilize the standard-mileage-rate method during the first year the automobile was placed in service and change methods in a later year to the actual-cost method, an accelerated method of depreciation cannot be used. You will have to use the straight-line method of depreciation over the useful life of the automobile.

The ***Standard-Mileage-Rate Method*** can only be utilized if you own the automobile being used for the benefit of the business, the automobile is not used for hire (Example: Taxi), and you are not operating two or more automobiles at the same time (Example: Fleet Operation). The standard-mileage-rate replaces all actual, fixed and depreciation expenses when determining the deductible business costs of operating a vehicle for business purposes. In other words, when you elect to utilize the standard-mileage-rate method, you will calculate the automobile expense by multiplying the total business miles driven by the IRS mileage allowance. The mileage allowance rate is set by the IRS, so be sure to check with the IRS to get the current mileage allowance rate for the current income tax year. *Now, any actual expenses such as gasoline, car repairs, depreciation, etc.*

*are not considered under this method. Reason being, the IRS mileage allowance is set to incorporate any such expenses. However, if you use the standard-mileage-rate method, you can deduct parking fees and tolls incurred during business use of the automobile.*

The *Actual-Cost Method* allows you to deduct the actual expenses, including depreciation, of operating an automobile for the benefit of your business. Therefore, if the automobile is used exclusively (100%) for the benefit of the business, all its operating costs may be deducted as automobile expenses. However, if the automobile is used for both business and personal use, you must separate the business use from the personal use. Operating costs include gasoline, oil, washing, repairs & maintenance, insurance, tires, supplies, etc. It is important to maintain accurate expense records when operating an automobile for the benefit of your business because you must substantiate these expense deductions with sufficient oral or written cvidcncc. When dealing with mileage, it is best to purchase a mileage book and keep accurate records of the miles driven for business use. With operating costs, it is best to keep track of all expenses (gas, repairs, supplies, etc.). If you are utilizing the standard-mileage-rate method, in reference to commuting, *you cannot deduct the cost of driving from your residence (home)* to your place of business or employment. However, once you have commuted to your place of business, you can deduct the mileage expense you incur from commuting from your place of business to conduct business or to other places of business.

## BAD DEBT

If you are owed money you cannot collect, you have a bad debt. Now, there are two types of bad debts, business bad debts and non-business bad debts. Since this manual pertains to business, we will focus on the business bad debts. In order for a bad debt to be deductible as a business expense, first of all, it had to have been incurred because of a business transaction. Second, the income from that transaction had to have been included in your business income previously. Therefore, if you are on the cash method of accounting, you cannot deduct a bad debt because the income was never reported. Remember, under the cash method of accounting business income is considered earned income once you have received the payment. Therefore, you do not have to report income you have not received under the cash method. So, since the uncollected bad debt was previously added to your business gross income, to deduct a bad debt expense, you simply deduct the amount of the bad debt from your current business gross income when figuring your business taxable income for the current tax year.

# CHARITABLE CONTRIBUTIONS

Charitable contributions are not always deductible as a trade or business expense. For example, if you make a charitable contribution with a *"charitable intent",* you may not be able to deduct that contribution as a business expense. However, if you make a charitable contribution that is in direct relationship with your business and this contribution is made with a *reasonable expectation* of a financial gain, then that contribution to the charitable organization is fully deductible as a business expense. Otherwise, the charitable contribution may be able to be deducted as an itemized deduction on Form Schedule A.

# DEPRECIATION EXPENSE

The rules and regulations regarding depreciation are complex. Explaining depreciation itsclf could easily fill several manuals. However, because of its importance in regard to your trade or business, this should at least give you an understanding of both its complexities and its importance.

Depreciation in its most simplistic explanation is a way of recapturing the cost of an asset (car, equipment, furniture & fixtures, etc.) over a specific period of time. In regard to the laws of taxation, the type of asset is what determines its useful life or the number of years the asset has to be depreciated before its value is considered fully exhausted. For example, in reference to taxation, an automobile's useful life is five years, whereas the useful life of furniture & fixtures is considered to be seven years. Therefore, an automobile has to be depreciated over a period of at least five years and furniture & fixtures has to be depreciated over a period of at least seven years. The method of depreciation is another area that takes serious consideration. There are several methods of depreciation you can choose from (Straight Line, ACRS, MACRS, Double Declining Balance, etc.). The objective is to utilize the method which will yield the greatest deduction.

Remember depreciation is an expense and requires serious consideration as well as knowledge of the rules and regulations governing its use. If you are the least bit unsure of the rules governing the depreciation of an asset used in your business, please seek assistance from a tax professional.

## EDUCATIONAL EXPENSES

Educational expenses have to meet one of two criteria before they can be deducted as business expenses. The two criteria are as follows:

1.) The expense has to maintain or improve skills required by the taxpayer in his or her employment, trade, or business, ***or***

2.) The expense must meet the express requirements of his or her employer, or the requirements of applicable law or regulations, imposed as a condition of the individual's retention of his or her salary, status, or employment.

Educational expenses include amounts spent for tuition, books, and similar items. They also include tutorial instruction, formal training, and seminars. It is important to note here that educational expenses that qualify you for a new business are not deductible as a business expense for your current business. The educational expense has to be beneficial to you in the performance of your business to be considered a deductible educational expense.

## EQUIPMENT EXPENSES

The cost of equipment used to produce income for your business is deductible as a business expense. As long as the equipment is used totally (100%) for your business, 100% of the costs related to the purchase and use of the equipment are totally deductible. However, if the equipment is also used for personal reasons, that part allocated to personal use is not a business deduction. Depending on the type of equipment and the cost of the equipment, a depreciation deduction may be necessary.

# HOME (BUSINESS USE OF HOME)

To deduct expenses for the use of your home in your business, a part of your home must be used regularly and exclusively as:

1.) The principal place of business for any trade or business in which you engage; or

2.) The place where you meet and deal with your patients, clients, or customers in the normal course of your trade or business; or

3.) In connection with your trade or business if you use a separate structure that is not attached to your home.

The amount you are allowed to deduct is based upon the percentage of your home you utilize for business. To compute the percentage, you can divide the number of square feet used for business by the total square footage of your home. Or, if the rooms are close in size, divide the number of rooms used for business by the total number of rooms in your home. From this point, the business expense portion can be computed by multiplying the percentage by the total of each expense. If you are utilizing both your home and another location regularly for business, you must decide which location is your principal place of business. To make this determination, there are two primary factors. One factor is the amount of time spent at each location and the second factor is the relative importance of the activities you performed at each location.

You cannot deduct the cost of lawn care maintenance for your home as a business expense; however, you can include as business expenses the business portion of mortgage interest, real estate taxes, utilities, depreciation, insurance, painting and repair for the portion utilized for business, rent and casualty losses.

## INSURANCE EXPENSES

The insurance premiums paid on fire and casualty insurance *(flood, burglary, hail, use and occupancy, etc.)* is a deductible business expense as long as the property is used in the business. *Life Insurance Premiums* paid by you for insurance on your own life are considered personal expenses and are not deductible as business expenses. However, if your business offers any type of life, medical or dental insurance coverage to its employees, the expense the company incurs as a result of these plans is deductible as a business expense.

## LEGAL AND PROFESSIONAL EXPENSES

Legal and professional fees that are in connection with your business are ordinarily deductible as business expenses. The criteria for deciding if legal and professional expenses are deductible are pretty much the same as those for *"ordinary and necessary"* business expenses. For example, hiring an accountant to keep your books, or a tax expert to prepare the tax return for your business are both examples of professional expenses and are both deductible as business expenses. An example of a legal expense is if an attorney is hired for concerns that originated in your business.

## MEALS AND ENTERTAINMENT EXPENSES

Both meals, and entertainment, are subject to a 50% limit. This means that only 50% of your meals and entertainment expenses are deductible *once the determination has been made that the expenses are deductible as business expenses* (Example: Meals & Entertainment Expense = $100.00; Solution $100.00 times 50% = $50.00; Meals & Entertainment Expense Deduction = $50.00). All though meals and entertainment expenses are subject to a 50% deduction limit, in order to be deducted as business expenses, they must still be *"ordinary and necessary"* expenses and they must have been incurred with the expectation of generating income for your business. Just having lunch does not constitute a business deduction, however having lunch with a prospect or a client with the intent of generating income for your business does.

To deduct meals or entertainment expenses, you must show that the activity was related to or associated with the active conduct of your business. There must be a clear business purpose for incurring the expense. As for meals, you can either keep records of your meal expense to deduct the actual cost or you can utilize the standard meal allowance, set by the IRS, which ranges from $30.00 to $42.00 per day depending upon when and where you travel.

## RENTAL EXPENSES

Rental expenses are deductible as business expenses if they meet the following criteria:

1.) The expense is incurred as a condition to the continued use or possession of property used by the taxpayer in a trade or business, and

2.) Neither the title nor the equity in the property is taken, nor has it been taken by the taxpayer.

The renting of space for you to operate your business is a deductible rental expense. The cost of renting equipment for you to utilize in your business is also a legitimate business expense.

## REPAIRS AND MAINTENANCE EXPENSES

Repairs and Maintenance Expenses are deductible if they are in connection with your business. The repair and maintenance of property and equipment used in the generation of income for your business is a legitimate business deduction. However, if the repair increases the life expectancy of the asset, a form of depreciation may be necessary. Replacing some shingles on a roof may not necessarily add to the life expectancy of the roof but replacing the entire roof does.

## SUPPLIES EXPENSE

The term *"Supplies"* covers a broad range. However, one rule to remember is that as long *as the supplies are for the use of your business, it is a legitimate business expense.* Of course, these expenses still have to be considered *"ordinary and necessary"* expenses. Some examples of supplies are office supplies, building supplies, etc.

## TRAVEL EXPENSES

The general rule to remember about travel expenses is *a deduction is allowed for traveling expenses while you are away from your tax home only if you are conducting business relevant to your business and you are required to be away from your tax home for a period of time longer than a day's work and sleep or rest is required so that you can meet the demands of the work required.* In addition, the expenses must again be *"ordinary and necessary."*

According to the tax rules, the city or general area in which your main place of business is located is considered your tax home. This is true regardless of the city or general area in which you and your family reside. For example, you and your family reside in Charleston, South Carolina but you work in Charlotte, North Carolina where you stay in a hotel and eat in restaurants. On the weekends, you return to Charleston, South Carolina to be with your family. You cannot deduct any travel expenses because for income tax purposes, Charlotte, North Carolina is considered your tax home. In addition, you also cannot deduct any of the expenses when you travel back to Charleston, South Carolina because the expenses are not business related. If by chance, you work in two or more areas; your tax home will be the area where your main place of business or work is located. There are wide ranges of expenses that qualify as travel expenses. In addition to expenses such as airfare costs, taxicabs, and other costs related to transportation, there are expenses such as hotel costs and parking, and tips that are incidental to any of the above expenses.

## UNIFORMS AND SPECIAL CLOTHING

The cost and upkeep of uniforms and special clothing could be allowed as a trade or business expense if it meets the following three criteria:

1) The uniforms or clothing are required as a condition of

employment,

2.) The uniforms or clothing are not adaptable to general wear, *and*

3.) The uniforms or clothing are not worn as general wear.

The cost and upkeep of uniforms and special clothing also include the laundering and cleaning of said clothing. As stated earlier, *the clothing must not be of the type, which is adaptable to ordinary wear.*

## WAGES AND PAYROLL

Employees bring about a whole new set of responsibilities and liabilities not to mention expenses. Properly withholding, depositing, and reporting payroll taxes are of the utmost importance. Businesses have been shutdown by the Internal Revenue Service due to not properly withholding, depositing, and reporting payroll taxes. The following information will take the guesswork out of the responsibilities of properly withholding, depositing, and reporting payroll taxes.

## WAGES AND PAYROLL

As a sole proprietor, you are required to pay your taxes quarterly in the form of *estimated taxes payments* during, or by the end of the month following the end of the quarter *(lst Quarter = Jan, Feb, Mar: Due Date  Apr. 30; 2nd Quarter = Apr, May, Jun: Due Date July 31;*

*3rd Quarter = Jul, Aug, Sep: Due Date Oct. 31; 4th Quarter = Oct, Nov, Dec: Due Date Jan.* 31). Because you cannot withhold payroll taxes on yourself, these estimated tax payments should be submitted along with the Form 1040ES (Federal) and with whatever form is required by the state in which you are conducting your business. If quarterly estimated tax payments are not made, you could find yourself paying a penalty for failing to pay estimated taxes. Since there is no employer to match the social security (FICA and MEDICARE) taxes, you are required to pay the entire amount yourself in the form of a self-employment tax which is calculated based on the net profit from your business during the filing of your income tax return.

If by chance you have employees, you are required to withhold payroll taxes, make deposits, and file quarterly reports. In reference to making payroll deposits, the amount of taxes withheld from your cmploycces' wages is the determining factor regarding when the deposits must be made. *Remember, as an employer, you have the responsibility of matching the social Security and Medicare taxes withheld from your employees' wages.* The penalties for failing to make employment tax deposits or for making your employment tax deposits late could be severe depending upon the amount of your employment tax liability. Again, the social security and Medicare taxes have to be matched by the employer. The social security tax is for old age, survivors, and disability insurance, whereas the Medicare tax is for hospital insurance. The Tax percentage rates for the social security and Medicare taxes are 6.2% for social security, and 1.45% for the Medicare tax.

There is a wage limit subject to the social security tax that changes annually, therefore please check with the IRS for the current social security wage limit. For Medicare, all wages are subject to the Medicare tax. In other words, once the employee's wages have reached the social security wage limit, the social security tax no longer has to be withheld. Since there is no cap on wages for the Medicare tax, it will continue to be withheld regardless of the amount of wages. Along with the deposit of taxes withheld from employees' wages, you must also make the required Federal Unemployment Tax deposits and payments. The Federal Unemployment Tax is calculated on the first $7,000.00 of each employee's wages. There may also be a required state unemployment tax requirement depending upon the state in which you are conducting your business.

## **PAYROLL REPORTS AND FORMS**

There are a number of payroll reports and forms an employer is responsible for submitting. By the end of the month following the end of the quarter *(lst Quarter = Jan, Feb, Mar: Due Date Apr. 30; 2nd Quarter = Apr, May, Jun: Due Date July 31; 3rd Quarter = Jul, Aug, Sep: Due Date Oct. 31; 4th Quarter = Oct, Nov, Dec: Due*

*Date Jan.* **31)** employers are required to submit a Form 941 (Employer's Quarterly Federal Tax Return). The Form 941 reports all federal income taxes, social security, and Medicare taxes withheld and deposited during the quarter. This form is automatically sent to you from the Internal Revenue Service. The Internal Revenue Service becomes aware of your status by the submission of your Form SS-4. If you have an employee or employees and do not receive your Form 941 via the mail, contact the Internal Revenue Service immediately. The number for the Internal Revenue Service is 1-800-829-1040.

The Form nine-forty is utilized to report the Federal Unemployment Tax paid during the quarter. This tax, along with the state unemployment tax, exists to provide payments of unemployment compensation to individuals who have lost their jobs. Most employers pay both the Federal Unemployment Tax and the state unemployment tax. The deposit for the Federal Unemployment Tax also has to be made by the end of the month following the end of the quarter. The Federal Unemployment Tax liability is determined by multiplying the amount of wages paid to each employee during the quarter by your Federal Unemployment Tax percentage. This tax is calculated on each employee and is done on each employee's wages up to $7,000. Once the employee's wages reach $7,000, the Federal Unemployment Tax liability stops for that employee. The Federal Unemployment Tax deposit coupons are also automatically sent to you via the mail from the Internal Revenue Service.

The state unemployment tax is also due by the end of the month following the end of the quarter. The contribution rate for the state unemployment tax varies. When a business submits its paperwork to the State Unemployment Insurance Agency to apply for a withholding number, the business is assigned a number as well as a contribution rate. If you have any questions, for your convenience a complete listing of the state unemployment insurance agencies has been provided in the back of the manual. The listing includes the address, phone number, and the email address of the agency.

## PAYROLL TAX DEPOSITS

Employers must deposit federal income taxes withheld, state income taxes withheld where applicable, the employee social security and Medicare taxes, and the employer's matching funds for the social security and Medicare taxes. Payroll tax deposits are made by depositing the appropriate funds at a financial institution that is an authorized depository for Federal taxes. If you are unsure, ask your banker if the institution is an authorized depository for Federal taxes. The deposits are made using the Form 8109 Federal Tax Deposit Coupon. New employers usually receive their coupon book from the Internal Revenue Service within 5 to 6 weeks after receiving an employer identification number. If you have not received your preprinted Form 8109 by the time you are required to make your first deposit, a Form 8109 B, which is an over-the-counter version of the Form 8109, can be utilized. However, by no means should you make deposits at an authorized depository if you have not received your employer identification number from the Internal Revenue Service. Your payment should be made payable to the "United States Treasury" and write on it your name (as shown on the SS-4), address, kind of tax, period covered, and the date you applied for your employer identification number. Do not use the Form 8109 B in this situation.

There are taxpayers that are required to electronically deposit their tax payments by using the Electronic Federal Tax Deposit System (EFTPS) in 2002. These taxpayers are identified by two factors:

1.) If the total tax deposits of such taxes in 2000 were more than $200,000 or
2.) If the taxpayer was required to use EFTPS in 2001.

If you are not required to deposit electronically, you can volunteer to do so. To receive more information, or to enroll in EFTPS, call 1-800-555-4477 or 1-800-945-8400. It is important that deposits are made timely. An employer is required to deposit 100% of the tax liability on or before the deposit due date (Accuracy of Deposit Rule). However, if the employer fails to deposit less than 100%, no penalty will be accessed if the following 2 conditions are met:

1.) A deposit shortfall does not exceed the greater of $100 or 2% of the amount of taxes otherwise required to be deposited and

2.) The deposit shortfall is paid or deposited by the shortfall date as described below.

**Makeup Date for Deposit Shortfall**

1.) **Monthly schedule depositor.** Deposit the shortfall or pay it with your return by the due date of the Form 941 for the quarter in which the shortfall occurred. You may pay the shortfall with Form 941 even if the amount is $2,500 or more.

2.) **Semiweekly schedule depositor.** Deposit by the earlier of:
   a.) The first Wednesday or Friday that falls on or after the 15th of the month following the month in which the shortfall occurred or
   b.) The due date of Form 941 (for the quarter of the tax liability).

**Your payment may be made along with the Form 941 if:**

1.) If your total taxes after adjustments and credits (line 12) are less than $2,500 for the current quarter or the prior quarter, and you didn't incur a $100,000 next-day deposit obligation during the current quarter, you don't have to make a deposit. To avoid a penalty, you will need to pay the amount in full with a timely filed Form 941 or you must deposit the amount timely. If you're not sure your total tax liability for the current quarter will be less than $2,500 (and your liability for the prior quarter wasn't less than $2,500), the IRS recommends that you make deposits using the semiweekly or monthly rules, so you won't be subject to failure-to-deposit penalties.

2.) You are a monthly scheduled depositor and make a payment in accordance with the Accuracy of Deposits Rule.

## Monthly Depositor:

You are considered a monthly depositor for a calendar year if the total taxes on your Form 941 (line 11) for the four quarters in your look back period totaled $50,000 or less. Being a monthly depositor; your payroll tax deposits have to be made by the 15th day of the next month. For example, when the month ends on January 31, the tax deposit has to be made no later than by February 15th. **(Note: The look back is a four-quarter period that begins on July 1 and ends on Jun 30.)**

## Semiweekly Depositor:

You are considered a semiweekly depositor for a calendar year if the total taxes on your Form 941 for the four quarters in your look back period totaled more than $50,000. Being a semiweekly depositor; your payroll tax deposits have to be made by the following Wednesday if the payday falls on a Wednesday, Thursday, or Friday, and by the following Friday if the payday falls on a Saturday,

Sunday, Monday, or Tuesday. **(Note: The look back is a four-quarter period that begins on July 1 and ends on Jun 30.)**

### $100,000 Next-Day Deposit Rule:

If you accumulate a tax liability of (reduced by any advanced Earned Income Payments) $100,000 or more during a deposit period, your payroll tax deposit must be made the next banking day regardless of whether you are a monthly or semiweekly depositor. Penalties may apply if the required deposits are not made on time. If the failure to make a proper and timely deposit was due to a reasonable cause and not willful neglect, the penalties will not apply. The penalty rates for not making deposits timely or properly are:

1.) 2% - Deposits made 1 to 5 days late.

2.) 5% - Deposits made 6 to 15 days late.

3.) 10% - Deposits made 16 or more days late. Also applies to amounts paid within 10 days of the date of the first notice the Internal Revenue Service sent asking for the tax due.

4.) 10% - Deposits made at an unauthorized financial institution, paid directly to the Internal Revenue Service, or paid with your tax return.

5.) 10% - Amounts subject to electronic deposit requirements but not deposited using EFTPS.

6.) 15% - Amounts still unpaid more than 10 days after the date of the first notice the Internal Revenue Service sent asking for the tax due or the day on which you receive notice and demand for immediate payment, whichever is earlier.

## WHO IS AN EMPLOYEE?

In general, as an employer, you have to withhold income taxes, withhold, and pay social security and Medicare taxes, and pay the appropriate unemployment taxes on wages paid to your employee or employees. If you classify an individual as an independent contractor and during an audit, the Internal Revenue Service deems the individual an employee and reclassifies the individual as an employee, you will become liable for all payroll taxes that were not withheld and paid plus whatever penalties and interest are appropriate. Therefore, it is important that you understand what the Internal Revenue Service looks at when determining the employment status of an individual.

In general, an individual who performs services for you is considered your employee if you can control what will be done, and the method in which it will be done. This is the case even if the individual is given freedom of action. In other words, the employer need not exercise control over the manner in which the work is performed, the mere fact that the employer has the right to control the employee when it is appropriate and deemed necessary is all that is required to meet the qualification of control. It is extremely important that the absence of the need to control the manner in which the individual performs his or her duties is not confused with the absence of the **right** to control.

There are at least four tests that are utilized to determine the status of an individual. They include: (1) the "common law employee" test, (2) the "20 factor" test, (3) the "7 factor" test, and (4) the" 12 factor" test.

**The "common law employee" test** is one of the most frequently used tests by the **IRS** and the tax courts. This test basically deals with the issue of the right-to-control in reference to the employer-employee relationship.

**The IRS "20 factor" test** was developed "as an aid in determining whether an individual is an employee under the common law rules." *Revenue Ruling* 87- 41. The 20 factors are as follows:

1. Instructions - An individual who has to comply with instructions about when, where, and how to work is ordinarily an employee.
2. Training - Training of an individual by an experienced employee or by other means is a factor of control and indicates an employee status.
3. Integration - Integration of an individual's services into the business operations generally displays that the individual is subject to direction and control and is therefore an employee.

4. <u>Services Rendered Personally</u> - If the services must be provided by the individual personally, it may suggest an employer-employee relationship. Normally when an individual is self-employed, he or she has the right to hire a substitute without the employer's knowledge.

5. <u>Hiring, supervising, and paying assistants</u> - Hiring, supervising, and payment of assistants by an employer normally indicates that the workers on the job are employees.

6. <u>Continuing relationship</u> - If after the individual has performed the required services the existence of a continuing relationship between the individual and the company or organization develops, this may indicate an employer-employee relationship.

7. <u>Set hours of work</u> - The establishment of set hours to work by the employer is an indication of an employer-employee relationship.

8. <u>Full time required</u> - If the employer establishes the worker must devote full-time to the business, the worker is ordinarily an employee.

9. <u>Performing the work on the employer's premises</u> - Performing the job on the employer's premises may indicate an employee status especially if the work can be performed somewhere else.

10. <u>Order or sequence of working</u> - If the employer controls the sequence or order of the work being    performed, this indicates employee status.

11. <u>Oral or written report</u> - If the employer requires the worker to submit written or oral reports regularly, an employer-employee

relationship may exist.

12. <u>Payment by hour, week, or month</u> - Employees are normally paid by the hour, week, or month.

13. <u>Payment of business expenses </u>- If the employer pays the worker's business or travel expenses, an employer-employee relationship may exist.

14. <u>Furnishing of tools and materials </u>- When an employer furnishes the tools and materials, this indicates an employer-employee relationship.

15. <u>Significant investment</u> - The employer furnishing all the necessary equipment and premises displays an employer-employee relationship.

16. <u>Realization of profit or loss</u> - Not being in a position to realize a profit or a loss indicates an employee status.

17. <u>Working for more than one firm at a time</u> - A self-employed individual usually works for more that one firm at a time.

18. <u>Making services available to the general public</u> - Normally, individuals who offer their services to the general public are self-employed.

19. <u>Right to discharge</u> - An employer normally cannot fire a self-employed individual as long as the work is being performed based upon the contractual agreement.

20. <u>Right to terminate</u> - Ordinarily an employee can terminate the relationship with an employer at any time without incurring liability.

## The Tax Court's "7 factor" test factors are as follows:

1. The degree of employer control over the worker,

2. Which party invests in the facilities utilized to perform the work,

3. The opportunity for profit or loss for the worker,

4. Whether the employer has the right to discharge the worker,

5. Whether the work being performed is a part of the employer's regular business,

6. The permanency of the relationship that exists between the employer and the worker,

7. The relationship the employer and worker believe they are creating.

## The Supreme Court's "12 factor" test factors are as follows:

1. The employer's rights regarding controlling the manner, in which the job will be performed and completed,

2. The source providing the tools and supplies that will be utilized to complete the work,

3. The location from which the work will be performed,

4. The duration of the relationship between the employer and the worker,

5. The employer's right to assign additional projects to the worker,

6. The employer's control regarding the amount of time it will take the worker to complete the job,

7. The payment method,

8. The employer's role regarding hiring the worker,

9. The employer's role in paying the worker,

10. Whether the work being performed is a part of the regular business of the employer,

11. Whether the employer is in business,

12. The benefits the worker receives.

## FAMILY EMPLOYEES

One of the perks of operating your own business is the ability to hire family members. If a child under the age of 18 works for his or her parents, payments received by the child for services rendered in the trade or business are not subject to social security and Medicare taxes if the business is a sole proprietorship or a partnership whereas the sole proprietor or the partners are the parents of the child. If one spouse employs the other, the wages paid for the services rendered by the employed spouse are subject to income tax withholding, social security, and Medicare taxes; however, the wages are not subject to Federal Unemployment Tax withholdings.

The wages paid to a child or a spouse for services rendered to the trade or business are subject to income tax withholding, social security, Medicare, and Federal Unemployment Tax if:

1.) A corporation, even if it is controlled by the child's parent or the individual's spouse,

2.) A partnership, even if the child's parent is a partner, unless each partner is a parent of the child,

3.) A partnership, even if the individual's spouse is a partner, or

4.)An estate, even if it is the estate of a deceased parent

## PAYMENTS TO NONEMPLOYEES

You are required to provide a Form 1099Misc to anyone you have paid at least $600 in rents, services, or other income payments. If the individual is not a corporation, the independent contractor should furnish a taxpayer identification number (Federal ID Number or Social Security Number) so a Form "ten-ninety-nine" Miscellaneous could be issued to the contractor by the business. Payments made to non-employees (Independent Contractors) are reported in box 7 of the Form "ten-ninety-ninc" Miscellaneous. Payments made to non-employees are characterized by four conditions:

1.) The payment is made to someone who is not an employee

2.) The payment is made for services in the course of a trade or business

3.) The payment is made to an individual, partnership, estate, or, in some

cases, a corporation; and

4.) The payment made to the payee is at least $600 during the year.

## BACKUP WITHHOLDINGS

It is extremely important for you to realize that if an independent contractor performs services and is paid at least $600.00 for the year, if that independent contractor is not a corporation, a taxpayer identification number should be furnished by the contractor, and a Form 1099 issued to the contractor by you. If the independent contractor fails to furnish you with a taxpayer identification number (Federal ID or Social Security Number), you are required by law to withhold 31 % of the amount of the compensation as "backup withholding." This should be done at the time of payment. After the payment has been made is too late.

## RECORD KEEPING

Income received by your business and the Expenses paid out by your business should be monitored and recorded. Utilizing a system that monitors your income and expenses is the first good step in developing an effective record keeping system. *As a taxpayer operating a business, it is your responsibility to maintain adequate records reflecting the day-to-day activities of your business.* You could pay an individual to maintain your accounting books or you can maintain your own books and seek advice when you have questions or need assistance. Although there is no particular method you have to utilize for bookkeeping, the method you do utilize must clearly reflect your business income and expenses.

All records related to your business activities such as receipts, cancelled checks, and other records that reflect income and expense information should be kept, at least, until the statute of limitation for that return expires. This is typically three years from the date the return was filed, or two years from the date the tax was paid, whichever is later. If you have employees, employment records must be kept for at least four years after the tax is due or paid, whichever is later. On a general note, income tax returns should be kept for at least three years. I recommend keeping your records indefinitely. It is always better to be safe than sorry.

Should you hire someone to maintain your accounting books is a decision you will have to make. However, your knowledge of that task and definitely your business structure and size of your business play a vital part in the decision. Records should be kept for at least four years, and available for IRS review. These records should include, but are not limited to:

1. Your employer identification number.
2. Amounts and dates of all wages, annuity, and pension payments.

3. Names, addresses, social security number, and occupations of employees and recipients.

4. Any employee copies of Form W 2 that were returned to you as undelivered.

5. Dates of employment.

6. Periods for which employees and recipients were paid while absent due to sickness or injury and the amount and weekly rate of payments you or third-party payers made to them.

7. Copies of employees' and recipients' Income tax withholding allowance certificates (Form W4, W4P, W4S, and W4V).

8. Dates and amounts of tax deposits you made and acknowledgement numbers for deposits make by EFTPS.

9. Copies of returns filed, including 941 TeleFile Tax Records and confirmation numbers.

## REIMBURSEMENT PLANS

There are two types of reimbursement plans I want to bring to your attention. One is an Accountable Plan and the other is a Non-accountable Plan. The Accountable plan requires the employee to meet all three of the following rules:

1.) The employee must have paid or incurred deductible expenses while performing services as your employee.

2.) The employee must adequately account to you for these expenses within a reasonable period of time.

3.) The employee must return any amounts in excess of expenses within a reasonable period of time. Under a non-accountable plan, payments to an employee for travel or necessary business expenses are treated as wages, and are subject to income, social securing, Medicare, and FUTA withholdings. Payments are treated as paid under a non-accountable plan if:

1. The employee is not required to or does not substantiate timely those expenses to you with receipts or other documentation or

2. You advance an amount to an employee for business expenses and the employee is not require to or does not return timely any amount he or she does not use for business expenses.

In general, an Accountable reimbursement plan would be best. With the Accountable reimbursement plan, the reimbursed funds are not treated as income. The expenses are generally the expenses of the business, and the business is just reimbursing the individual. Unlike the non-accountable reimbursement plan whereas the funds advanced to an employee for travel or necessary business expenses are treated as wages, and are subject to income, social security, and Medicare taxes withholdings.

# AUDITING PROCEDURES

During an audit, an auditor gathers what are called *"samples."* A sample can be any part and any portion of your financial records. The auditor uses these samples to test the validity of your financial records regarding accuracy and truthfulness. Because you will have no idea where the samples will be pulled and tested, it is important that all of your financial records be accurate and in order.

The Internal Revenue Code, Paragraph 7602 gives the IRS authority to conduct audits of persons or organizations to:

1. Determine the correct amount of taxable income if any,
2. Make a return where none has been filed,
3. Determine the liability of any person or organization for any Federal tax, and
4. To collect taxes owed to the federal government.

Listed below are a few areas the IRS may check during an audit.
1. Financial records and bank statements,
2. Administrative files,
3. Personnel files,
4. The governing documents (Articles of Incorporation, by-laws, Minutes, etc.),
5. Contracts,

6. Audit of all **responsible parties'** individual income tax returns for the same years in question as the business.

7. Income tax returns

## RETIREMENT PLANNING

Retirement is a part of life we all should prepare for and the earlier we begin to prepare the better. Being self-employed, your social security taxes are paid and collected in the form of self-employment taxes. However, relying just on social security for retirement may not be a wise decision. Just as tax planning and strategy do not begin during the income tax preparation stage, so it is with planning for retirement. Planning for retirement should begin in the early stages of one's life and continues until the age of retirement. It should not begin at the age of retirement or a few years before the age of retirement.

A qualified retirement plan allows the reporting of income to be deferred until retirement while allowing the contributions to be currently deducted. In other words, you do not pay any income taxes on the part of your income contributed to a qualified retirement plan. In addition, you are allowed to claim a deduction for the contributions made to the qualified retirement plan in the year in which the contributions were made. For the purpose of participating in a qualified retirement plan, self-employed individuals (sole proprietors, partners in a partnership or members of an LLC) are treated as employees even if the self-employed individual has employees.

Although there are several forms of retirement plans for self-employed individuals, for simplicity's sake, I will address just two types. These two types are the *Keogh plan, and the Simplified Employee Pension Plan.* Because self-employed individuals are treated as employees regarding contributing to one of these qualified retirement plans, not only will you be planning for retirement, *but you will also be reducing your current income tax liability as well.* Although there are contribution limitations, the tax savings would still be rather significant. The Keogh and Simplified Employee Pension Plan retirement plans are just two of several retirement plans that can be utilized by self-employed individuals. There are other plans you should research and become familiar with. This section was included to express the importance of planning for retirement and for presenting a foundation or direction from which you may start. The rules and regulations governing qualified retirement plans are complex and proper structuring is important therefore, for assistance or guidance please do not hesitate to consult a professional.

When hiring independent contractors, in order to avoid complications, the contract should incorporate the following 10 pieces of information clearly and be recorded in writing between the employer and contractor.

1.) The worker is an independent contractor not an employee.

2.) The worker is restricted from holding out as an employee.

3.) The contractor has the right to control the project.

4.) Terms for either party terminating the arrangement are outlined, including consequences of termination.

5.) The contractor is exempt from all employee benefits.

6.) The contractor is responsible for accounting of all taxes.

7.) If the arrangement is for ongoing services, a specific term subject to renewal is provided.

8.) When possible, the contractor pays all out-of-pocket expenses for work on a project.

9.) When possible, payment is provided on a per-project basis.

10.) Where feasible, contractor will provide tools and equipment necessary to complete the job.